It's a terrible thing that we are taught to identify ourselves
with things and identities.
It's a huge burden!

Happiness has very little to do with material things.
Find your connection with the self and learn to live happily.

Learn to Live for Yourself

By Dimple Ahluwalia

A Subtle Journey towards Self Realisation

All ideas and thoughts are experimental.
They are not meant to offend anyone person, religion or community.

Contents

Contents

Contents

Introduction

This book is my thoughts that I want to convey to myself because I have led a peculiar life inspite of being totally clear in my heart and mind. The bubble of the world is so intense and huge in magnitude that it engulfs you, no matter how hard one tries to stay uninvolved.

The content of this book is more conversational towards the reader and it may land differently on everyone's ears. The views are only mine and I certainly do not expect everybody to agree with them. Yet, there will be those who may find resonance. So not giving any extra importance to be understood by all but to find my tribe who struggles to make connections because they find themselves totally out of sync with the worldly ways. I am keeping a carefree attitude because this book is meant to make me unload all of the toxic ways that are built by society to control a human being.

I have come to understand that all relationships are illusory and we indulge, either to fulfil a deep need inside us or just for the sake of entertainment or timepass. Some individuals disguise their intentions in the garb of juicy words and make you fall with their false narratives.
My endeavour has always been to not buy into a culture that tries to dictate and tame anyone.

About Me

I love experimenting with life and look at it as an experience to be had and not a story to be told. If we make our life into a story then we will take everything personally and that's the biggest cause of sadness. I learnt very early in life that fame, success or achievements are the world's way to use you for its benefit. That is just the nature of outward success.

I am a meditation enthusiast and have guided several people from all age groups, genders and communities to help them get connected with their inner being, and all participants resulted in being happier and claim that their lives changed for better.

Art excites me to the point of ecstasy, I can find art in the water spilled on floor or the flaky paint on a wall.
Digitech has changed my life because I am a homebody and it gives me the luxury to explore the world without losing my connection with myself and take my voice out there without making myself go through unnecessary hassles.

I love my life and write to convey a message of relaxation to people, because everyone seems to be in a great hurry.

I urge you to enjoy your life, because it's here today and gone tomorrow, so ephemeral!

A Message to my Readers

It's a long journey to take, you need to unpack a lot of unnecessary baggage before you pack the essentials.

It is extremely crucial to make a new world which is a safer place than we landed in. Let's make it a personal mission to work on ourselves a little bit every day to be more empathetic and compassionate towards our own inner being. Give yourself everything you need. And that will be enough.

Thank you for doing your part. You are a reason this world is a better place and people continue to believe in kindness.

Preface

The current culture is producing diseased, unhappy and extremely greedy individuals. A highly stressful home, work and social environment is prevalent everywhere, seeping deeper into the nerves with each passing day. It is making people harmfully competitive, ready to tear one another down because every one feels less than the other but wants to be celebrated as the BEST.

No one understands that we are all the best in our unique ways. We forgot to be the leaders that we were born as and became slaves of the work culture, hence we have become competitors, rivals, enemies who can't participate in the success of another. The fake culture has made people isolate from their true meaningful purpose of life. The rise of psychosomatic disorders is a testament that everyone is walking unaware and doesn't know the cause of their despair despite achieving their goals, having relationships, friendships and all the material possessions touted to lead to a happily ever after.

My whole work is equal to a prayer encouraging world peace, but it will begin to show results only if I have peace in my mind, in my life. That goes for every single person out here on this earth.

An un peaceful person cannot recognise peace and will fight with it, looking at it like a stranger and will try to defeat it lest it destroy him. An unaware person will create more suffering for himself and the world around him because that's all he knows. Love, acceptance and happiness are alien concepts for him and he will reject them. That is the world we live in, full of tamed, weak, fearful, angry and hostile people who are at such a dis ease with themselves that they can convert any good situation into a threat and go to war with it.

Hypocrisy is prevalent in families, communities and the whole social structure. This is a serious cause of concern because it leads one to trust the wolf in a sheep's clothing.

Why are we so threatened by the abundance, beauty and success of another? We can be superficial but not authentic. What stops us from being genuinely happy for another?

Move Beyond Illusions and Claim your Freedom

The Struggles are for Real
And Heartbreaks are never Kind.

When the Days seem like Forever
And Smokey air fills the Night.

I know You need the Rest
You Blame Yourself for not Getting it Right.

I've been there too, Stayed and Yelled with all my Might.
Crying my Lungs Out, and sometimes Trembling Down
with Fright.

So, all I Want You to know is —
I See You .

You may want to stay Down and Under
BUT
Don't get Pulled Down for Longer.

In the Wheel of Life, Everything Comes and Goes, yet,
Nothing is a Blunder
There is much hurt and pain, also unlimited Fun and
Thunder.

None will stay past longer, if you don't hold on to it Tight.
Choose to loosen the reins on scars and Relish the Smiles
with Delight.

Once the dust begins to settle, know that you've put up a
great Fight.

Do not peek at the world from behind the curtains.
Do not hide behind those closed doors.

No matter what's going on in your life
You need to step out of your head.

You have to show what you are made of -
The Sun, The Fire and all things Glowing and Bright.

I am longing to see Your Face.

O' Dear now appear,
And Give me a glimpse of your Light!

My Commitment to Live for Myself

A Journey towards Self Realisation

Name :

____

____

____

Start Date :

____

____

My promise to myself :

____

____

01 Recognising the Trap

Life as we know it today, feels more like a grind, a series of goals to achieve, benchmarks to set, a perfect family to raise, material possessions to be had, accolades to gather and a to-do bucket list to tick on our timeline.

Is that all there is to do and live for? How much satisfaction is any human being feeling walking on the tightrope of this given format?

My guess is - very little to none!

Yet each one gets up daily and continues to do the same routine work and follow the same habits, have the same goals as dictated by the societal norm. The brains have become so habitual that the mind fails to see that it is being manipulated by what the eyes see around them, ears have gone deaf by the sound of fake success.

You want to do different things or maybe same things but differently, you know that you are stuck in the pattern but you end up second guessing your horrible feeling inside because you see others showing up in the same sorry story, complaining, yet not changing anything for themselves. The most you do is stop complaining, frustrate yourself even more and carry on with ticking one item after another from your to do list.

 Accomplishing the given tasks for the day is the biggest high of your life. Happiness, Satisfaction, Joy, Enthusiasm evade you. The same questions appear everyday, the same struggles and obstacles haunt your path periodically, yet you sit there wondering what is it that you are doing wrong.

Have you ever looked at it like - I am just in a maze created by someone else and like a rabbit I am trying to make my way through the labyrinth, so that I can finally reach my carrot. But, finally when I get to the prize, I am so depleted, tired, my spirit compromised and worn out, that the prize doesn't even feel worth all the work that I had put in and the mental struggle that I went through. To make things worse, the goal post has now shifted.

You are angrier and more frustrated than before!

Yet, you begin again, searching for a new carrot, perhaps this time you are a squirrel that is trying to secure it's future by running swiftly to gather all the nuts that will help you get by the rest of your life, adversities and all. It certainly has started occurring to the mind, that maybe it's the wrong way to be. Something feels unsettling in the gut and brings to light a pertinent question -

"Is it a Trap to keep me away from my real treasure?

"Yes", says a voice,

What do I do, so that I do not become a victim again?"

"All you have to do is - just get out of it." the voice responds again,

"It's an Illusion, created to keep you involved in the lower and menial activities so that you remain tamed and be a follower, at the most - leader of a pack of Idiots."

"Now that I see the trap, how do I not even enter through it's doorway, or at least get out of it while I still have time!?", I ask

Here is the answer,

"You must <u>want</u> to get out of it.
That is the first crucial decision to make."

"Once you recognise that you are in trap and this trap is
keeping you away from living your best life, all you have to do
is make the decision to just get out of it." the voice confirms

My Verdict:

Wake up

Shake Yourself off

Get out of it

It's all a Trap!

JOURNALING PROMPTS

Do you feel trapped in your life?

Can you recognise the traps?

How can you get out of these traps?

02 Staying longer than needed causes harm

Once you feel that happiness and joy have left your life, you will know you are stuck inside a trap. It's a confirmation!

When you are unable to see and find any hope existing in your life, you are continuously motivating yourself through the outer mediums - it's your sign that you are inside and everything else is on the outside.

You may sometimes feel a fleeting glimmer of relief by hearing an inspiring quote or a talk, and temporarily be motivated to take action but as soon as you try to take control to move forward, you are overcome with self doubt, anxiety and the knowledge of your own limitations. All the sets of "why's" stare at your face and you are stopped in your tracks.

Is this your own life anymore?

Every sphere of your life - personal or professional; every decision making capacity seems to have been hijacked!

Why does this happen?

Reasons:

You do not feel confident enough
It seems like a huge task to pursue your dreams and go for what you want. You doubt whether you even have it in you to consider that you deserve the life that you wish for or is it just wishful thinking on your part!

The reason you aren't confident is because you do not have the necessary skills. Gaining the expertise seems daunting. Would you be able to step up and put in the work?

Every new set up impacts our current situation. Pursuing your dreams may affect the relationships you have in your life. Will you end up neglecting your loved ones or will they be unhappy with you because you may not be able to give them the required time as usual.

All these above listed factors seem like too much and you end up choosing safety over a well calculated, deliberate action with preparedness in the direction of your choice.

You give up!
You stay back in the rut.
You stay in the trap longer than required, this causes harm.

JOURNALING PROMPTS

Have you stayed in the trap long enough?

___

WHAT ARE THE HARMS IT CAUSED YOU?

___

What are the reasons you stayed in the trap for so long?

___

03

Key is to Build Yourself up

Conquer all of your fears by ignoring the trap.
Chart your own path and single-mindedly walk in
that direction.

You are now somewhat familiar with the factors that define a trap

- The worldly goals that you have been asked to run after and achieve.

- The markers of success which are pre defined and the world assures you that it will honour you once you get to the finish line.

Do these outcomes ever come through?

Does the highest success when achieved, stay sustainable?

Does the next target not stand in front of you as soon as one is accomplished?

Everything involving such kind of achievements requires - an other.

For a happy relationship, you require an other to have a relationship with.

For the material success to be seen, you need material objects to showcase the success.

Now Consider :

How will you ever know what you really want when you are being continuously surrounded by manufactured information?

You see fake happy faces that mask their pain and you believe them.

Everyone is running the same race of pain, shame and overwork that amounts to no happiness, but no one wants to show their struggles and frustrations of being had by the world. Nobody wants to acknowledge that they wasted their precious time in such useless pursuits.

No one wants to point a finger, no one wants to find a way, so they succumb to the pressure and carry on living this laborious life.

Relevant points to ponder :

Are your life pursuits something that you want inherently or are they built upon the model that you see all around.

How can building a relationship with another, be the goal of your life when there is no control on the outcome that it will enhance your quality of life despite your best efforts.

Are the ultimate success markers even designed to bring peace, joy or satisfcation of any kind or are we being sold the harmful stuff.

The trap is harmful and disastrous

The damage of buying into this harmful trap is that, too much time is lost before you even recognise it. You have anger because you now realise that you have been manipulated. You do not know any other way so you are still running after the shiny stuff to make your life feel worth something.

You can run as much as you want after the close friendships you crave, the family you want to make, the lover you want to have, the opulent houses you want to own, the shiny car you want to drive, the private jet you want to fly in, the expensive diamonds you want to have on display, the satisfaction of owning any of these things never reaches your soul. Joy never even touches you, in fact, it is so short lived that you are already gunning for the next milestone. What you may have dealt in the process could spell like - the aftermath of back stabbing, deceit, manipulation, broken heart, scars and a lifetime of regret. You learn your lesson, make a resolve to never repeat it, yet you fall back into the same trap, because you do not know a way that leads to lasting happiness. On the contrary, you have made up your mind that this is the only way the world works and it's the only way to exist.

What you don't realise and open
your eyes to is the fact that -

You already have a golden life but
you are wasting every moment in
mulling over the small stuff. The
happy faces, the shiny diamonds,
the exorbitant mansions are all an
illusion, thus useless.
Do you realise that you will pay for
all this with - Your Life and Your
Joy.

JOURNALING PROMPTS

Do you believe in the world's definition of success?

What are the aspirations that are your own?

What is the path that you want to set for yourself that will give you satisfaction?

Man is the only creature who dares to go against nature, yet, going against the societal norm is much feared.

Man is the only creature that developed this world to make his life more comfortable, yet we discourage those who want to follow their bliss.

It's a terrible thing that we are taught to identify ourselves with things and titles.

I think it's the fearful ones who are running the race and the fearless ones are calling the shots on others.

Why would you choose keeping the house tidy and what people think of you over going for what makes your soul sing.

Do not go for any pursuit to find self worth or make an identity for yourself. Pursue and persevere to build yourself with characteristics that form your highest expression.

Success and failure are not scary words, instead they are your indicators whether you are on your path or someone else's.

Because there is no failure on your soul's path, the courage to start that journey in itself brings success, now and forever.

Also, you may now get closer to yourself and build a precious connection with someone who understands and supports you rather than force you to suppress any parts of you!

04 Finding your Real Essence

Do you know that the real you is someone beyond any of the roles you play and is always present within you, waiting for you to take the lead.

The real work of this life is much different and goes beyond being someone's son, daughter, husband, wife, brother, sister, employee or employer. But surprisingly you only know yourself as a person with your current name, age, gender, role and title.

If you have ever been in despair and cried, you would have experienced a knowing voice that speaks from the inside and guides you differently from the way you have lived your life. It asks you to leave it all, run away to the mountains, move cities, change your friends and family. It may even prod you to take on a new personality.

Who is this and what is it trying to show you? Is it your mind coming up with ways to escape an unhappy life or is it the larger dimension making itself seen to show you the possibilities beyond what you have experienced so far.

I am sure you have begun to understand where the content of this book is leading you towards. Through the medium of my words, my hope is to make you understand that you have authority on your life and you can begin to take the lead by listening to the personal inner voice of guidance.

Points to Remember

Life is not a duty, instead, life is a flow that emerges from the inside and wants to express itself out in the world. As opposed to the common view that life is given to us to attain everything from the outside, in reality life is given to connect with the inner flow and channel our treasures from the inside out. Whatever you crave for from the outside becomes a responsibility. Everything that is created from the inside becomes joy.

Responsibility	Ultimate Joy
Romantic love	Universal love
Relationships	Authenticity
Material possessions	Art, Music, Dance
Ambition	Consciousness

JOURNALING PROMPTS

Are you willing to find your true essence?

What are some of your natural ways of expressing joy?

Where do you feel the discomfort when you are not able to achieve worldly targets?

JOURNALING PROMPTS

How do you express your disappoints with yourself when you don't feel good enough?

In which roles do you feel tied?

Would you be willing to exchange some of your material possessions for spiritual joy?

05 Nurture Yourself Everyday

Where must you keep your attention so that you do not deviate from inner path and continue to make progress for your supreme satisfaction?

Yourself!

Instead of analysing the world and its reactions, keep your mind tuned to the inner self where only you exist in your pure form. The advantage of practising this is that your own reactions* will begin to subside when you do not give attention to anything and everything out there in the world. The people of the world and what they are doing is the main cause of distress for most humans because they are always connected with the outside world and keep judging everything that lands in their awareness . This is a sure shot way of always being out of tune with the self.

If you are easily irritable, know that your vision is set on the outside and you are in the trap and are harming yourself.

Break this type of reaction inducing input. If you are plugged in and centered, then there is very little that will disturb you.

Nurture yourself everyday to remain in touch with your inner most self and do all activities in the world from that point of synchrony . Every act you perform begins from a profound place from the inside and flows out into the world.

Earning money, having relationships, dealing with friends, family and all other obligations can be operated in the similar way. You will eventually notice that your life circumstance will appear to be improving. This is just your beginning towards a beautiful, satisfying and cherish-able life.

*reaction - when you re enact what has come towards you. e.g when someone yells, you feel disturbed and yell back, you only re enact, you are not exerting the power of your will on yourself, you just get pulled with the others' or the situation's energy.

JOURNALING PROMPTS

How often do you react to circumstances in a
calm manner in daily life?

While accommodating others in your life, do you
neglect yourself?

Do you recognise the emotional health of your
inner being? How is it currently?

JOURNALING PROMPTS

How can you engage with yourself more to strengthen your bond with the self?

Are you aware of the perception others have of you?

When do you care about the opinions of others in your life?

06

Failure is a way of Succeeding

Any path deviation along a life circumstance is not failure. On the contrary it is the dropping of the illusion of what you think will work for you.

We have been taught that success is only when everything works out in the way we plan for it to work out. It's notable at this point that if you don't criticise your strategy but relook at your intention, much will be revealed to you about yourself and the reasons why something did not work out for you in your desired manner.

But we are also inclined to blame the outside factors at this time, because everything is done for an outcome in the outer world. We haven't been taught to work from our authenticity, but from what is acceptable out there. As a result, when things or projects fail, we totally deny our part in the process, and it's true, because it was never something that came from our core desires.

If you continuously face redirection, you must understand you are working from the outside in. Dig, sieve, search inside all the veils that hide your true desires and authentic parts of yourself that you hide from your own self too because of the fear of rejection from the society. Once, all these veils are lifted and all masks dropped, you will unabashedly, unapologetically and without attaching any sense of shame, walk towards the direction that is truly yours and even if you tremble or live in humble means, you will be genuinely fulfilled, satisfied, overjoyed, ecstatic and inspirational to everyone who has the eyes to see your beauty.

But, the worldly outcome is not what you are living for. People will get inspired and appreciate you if they want to, worldly success will happen if it has to. That is not your goal.

Whatever you create from within is for you and through the making of it you are fulfilling your purpose and serving what you came for in the larger scheme of things. This is your role and not the one defined by society. Those roles are designed to keep you small and contained - but you are the wilderness!

Wilderness is where we belong!
It runs in our blood and in our thoughts.
It makes itself visible in all the actions we undertake.

Only when a human succumbs to a higher human authority,
does he become fearful and cautious of his deeds.

This fear does nothing for him but instils disease,
makes him accumulate what he actually came to release.

JOURNALING PROMPTS

Have you ever made decisions against the will of your near ones?

Do you have the courage to express your deeper desires with your dear ones?

How far can you go to achieve your worldly dreams? Can you do the same with your real desires?

07 The Divine Energy

A life lived beyond illusions is of the highest nature and amounts to the expression of divine energy flowing through you.
That's the Real You!

We all have a certain uniqueness within us. The way we walk around in the world and interact with the world is unique to us. The more we stay in line with what we truly want to express the faster we reach who we have the potential to be.

If a caterpillar decides to not go in the cocoon, because it wants to hang out with the other insects and be the cool one; if it doesn't follow it's natural path out of the fear of missing out; it decides to follow the other species that are only meant to devour the leaves and suck nectar from flowers for life , it will definitely not blossom to fly freely and be the attractive butterfly which it is destined to be!

Similarly many humans, like the disillusioned caterpillar are crawling all over the ground. Staying small, working overtime instead of doing what's necessary for their own growth because they are so separated from their inner core due to societal conditioning. They only know of existing inside limits than to go inward, strengthen themselves and come out strong, spreading their colourful wings and claiming their space in the universe.

What a dis service it is to oneself and the whole mankind that a beautiful essence which took shape of a living being did not prosper and become who it was wired to be, instead it gave in to the pressures of fitting in, being accepted by others and compromised on his own acceptance, love and joy!

Thoughts that keep you from flying high:

Lazy attitude

It's just one life to live, so why work hard.

Why do I need to do anything when everything is provided for me.

I will have to compromise on my time with friends or my relationship will suffer.

Negative judgement of success

Society doesn't approve of what I want to do, I want to fit in and don't want to do anything that is not allowed.

My ideas are weird, no one will relate with them.

Faulty perception

What can I achieve what others haven't already.

I will still be less richer and successful than my peers.

These attitudes sound like compromises on the self.

Such thoughts will keep you limited in happiness and personal satisfaction.

You will definitely miss out on your life that could have been - because excuses almost always refrain one from living freely in their true essence.

JOURNALING PROMPTS

Can you identify your unique gifts?

Do you give yourself excuses for making decisions which are not in alignment with your true self?

What is your personal happiness index?

08 Culture as a Concept

A culture is a set of cells that have similar traits, prosper in a certain environment and perpetuate with their best characteristics for their best fullest expression in the world and continue to do for generations what they have been programmed to, by nature.

We are familiar with the same concept of cultures and understand that humans also identify themselves with this idea. In any culture, all the new generations grow up like the previous ones. They maintain a certain order in their communities and provide the necessary conditions to produce the best off springs who will grow up to their best potential just as nature intended.

It is my idea that human beings come as sets, some portray the characteristics of cats, other dogs, some exhibit wolf like qualities, others are a snake or a lion. Some are birds, others butterflies, some belong to the species of predators, while others are vulnerable like preys.

The concept of culture is derived from the understanding that each human has unique set of qualities and are unchangeable by choice and a bad environment can totally mess up the future of these species.

A culture produces more of it's own, thats why cultures protect their own, guard their off spring from bringing anyone from a different culture so that their traits do not get diluted. Reproduction is also allowed with the like, cultures live in the same controlled environment for generations and flourish. All members feel safe, nurture each other because they understand each other totally. As a result, they grow to express their divine expression. But culture system has got violated over our history and the intermixing of diverse cultures has created a chaos, leading to confusion and downfall of human race.

It is not to say that diversity is not good, but in this context, belonging to a culture is more beneficial. Also, one culture is not better than the other, it's just that each one has its function in the bigger picture. Every culture prospers, with love and kindness towards others and does the best for a united world of togetherness. Separation is the first step towards bad times. Only if nature segregates, there can be a higher purpose towards such an act. Only nature has the power to dictate terms.

So you ask, what's my role in all this?
Your work is to get in touch with yourself, to find which culture you belong to, you will see that in real life you gravitate towards people who are suitable for you, who understand you and support you to live your best life. In turn you feel the same towards them also.

There is no missing piece you need to find to complete the puzzle for which you run through mazes all life long.

I invite you to take that inward journey, not in the hope of earning money, hitting any target or finding love in another human being. But to get closer to yourself. To let your hidden parts reveal themselves and then you can polish them for a shinier, brighter future.

You have incredible power to influence your own life.

JOURNALING PROMPTS

Who are some of the people you can relate with? Are they a part of your family?

Do you feel there is something missing in your life always?

Do you feel like the odd one out in any or many situations? List them.

09 Attachment & Detachment

Connection is the natural way to detachment and the end of suffering.

The mention of attachment theory in the spiritual realm largely pertains to the triggering of all emotions and outcomes that occur due to being overly attached to the self, relationships, money and titles. People who identify themselves with their role are totally attached and will undergo suffering from ego, anger etc at the slightest provocation. They will continue to perpetuate such scenarios in their life which will keep them stuck in these emotional cycles repeatedly.

The detachment theory is taught in order to save the human from disappointments, heartbreaks and let downs. Everything we do in the modern day world is to be successful, because that is what we have been taught to look for, whereas nothing called success and achievements exists. Detachment from the false accumulations will take you closer to your true self and build connection with the real being inside.

What really exists is connection and disconnection.

Our inflated ego because of the so called success and our anger because of the so called failure is nothing but our disconnect from who we really are and how we truly see ourselves.

What we truly believe about ourselves is that we want to be appreciated, loved and cherished. But we are conditioned to believe that we can have it all only if we fulfill the pre requisites dictated and demanded by the society. Our parents believed it too, so instead of loving us for who we are, they started to prep us for what the world appreciates.

Instead of giving us their love freely they put boundaries on it. What they gave us freely was not what we deserved but an illusion that if our comforts are withheld, we will strive to be better.
As children, we begin to believe what our parents said and thought about us.

Now we will only produce more from their negative reflection of our personality and keep suffering our whole lives, knowing we are not who our parents thought us to be but trying to prove otherwise. There is no end to this and the suffering continues. Ask the high achievers, record breakers, award winners if they will ever be satisfied. It's not themselves that each one is trying to satisfy, but its a perception of themselves that they are trying to influence for the world and their parents to see them in their true light. In their own heart they know their own tenderness, the purity of their soul and the fact that they do not need to work so hard, they are happy with the little things they have yet they will never be able to satisfy the world. All they get at the end of life is loneliness despite the worldly success.

The world will only worship the greatest they say, the greatest is not somewhere out there, it resides within you, I say. Right now, there is a lot of attachment with all things outward because there is a big disconnect from the self.

Attachment happens because of Disconnection
Detachment happens when there is Connection

We all are operating in this world from a lens of illusory perception and that is the cause of differences among people throughout the world.

How illusion can create chaos:

Mental Suffering

Those who live under a heavy veil of illusory perception have a stronger attachment and vice versa. They strongly judge the world and look at it as a dark, bad place and believe that here everyone is out to get everyone else.

Limited Mindset

Trauma forms a veil of illusion on perception, which in turn distorts reality and begins to convey every information from a past experience. The data for which was received from the outside. Such people are always overly cautious in personal life.

Hides Reality

Connection happens when you are aware enough to see all events as such and not attach any meaning to what you are going through or seeing around you in the context of feedback for your life, work or relationships. You do not get indoctrinated by what you see and understand that any reaction from you means you have got yourself caught in the web of illusion.

All these listed factors are hidden and may feel like too much for anyone to comprehend and one ends up choosing safety over a well calculated, deliberate action with preparedness in the direction of your choice.

One gives up, yet again!
As a result, one stays back in the trap.
Staying in the rut longer than required, causes harm. This is the time when self doubt and self deprecating may begin to find roots in the way one thinks and talks about oneself. I would like to offer a word of solace at this time, because this is some heavy stuff and has got so deeply ingrained as it is being reinforced, resounded and reverberates from all directions. That is why the importance of a Guru is so highly recommended in our culture. But if one gets silent and still enough, the inner Guru appears and helps cut through all illusions by reassuring that the feeling of anxiety, restlessness, sadness, frustration are true and are trying to communicate a need. The need of having courage to choose the path of one's soul's direction. That is where your prize awaits you in the form of satisfaction, equanimity and peace.

JOURNALING PROMPTS

Do you feel easy to give away your old items that you no longer use?

Do you identify yourself with how rich, good looking or successful you are?

How do you view the people in your circle and the world at large? List both.

10 Unconditional Love?

Something that every human craves secretly is unconditional love. That is the reason we are told it is found in a soulmate, abundant money, stupendous career and when one has had it all and yet not found unconditional love, spirituality becomes the answer. The market is ripe with selling unconditional love through self care routines, praying to God, yoga, meditation, climbing the highest mountain peaks. Alas! these practices also fail and thus are futile if you follow them solely for achievement or purpose of transaction.

Where is this one source that will continue to bestow it's blessings on me no matter how crazy or how unfriendly I am. Every relationship is transactional, even the one with an outer God. We are trying to impress everyone, be it a lover, a boss, social circle, or pursuing goals like work, hobbies, travelling and just about anything to get some results.

Have you ever tried offering yourself to yourself? Purely, for no reason, have you?

It's not in the shedding of the ego or becoming humble towards others, serving everyone out there or being sweet in our behaviour. No, these are all the wrong places to put yourself into and go seeking anything.

The only person who is capable of giving you never-ending, overflowing and abundant unconditional love under any and every circumstance is YOU.

Only if you understand that you will do everything in your life that you are asked to guard against and is labelled as a sin or unacceptable, regardless of what you have done, you have to embrace your own self and your experience of life. There alone lies the fountain of unconditional love.

Go drink from it and never ask or expect it from any outside source.

JOURNALING PROMPTS

Have you been able to give unconditional love to anyone?

How often have you been betrayed or had your heart broken by others?

Do you believe in destiny? Why or why not, list both.

The Next Step

There is a difference between having the markers of living well and actually living well. We all have seen accomplished grumpy people and carefree happy non identified with materialism people. The unhappy ones are those who bought into the trickery of the world and never feel enough about themselves or anything else in their lives, while those who chose to stay connected with their core being may not have the impermanent sources of happiness but they continue to drink from the cup of divine nectar and no one has the power to disturb their peace. They will soon catch up with the worldly success too and will still remain connected to the one that bestows!

Where do you belong?

If you are not truly living well everyday then how does accumulation of the badges or honours contribute to the quality of your life?

Understand the difference and live life with the RIGHT ATTITUDE.

To be truly happy in your life here, have gratitude towards all the people you encounter and all the experiences that you ever have - good, bad, ugly. Do not overindulge in them. Keep your one and only relationship with your inner being at the highest and see miracles unfold in front of your eyes everyday.

Surrender yourself to the inner guidance and stop waiting for results, because what you await in the end is the illusion, how you begin and move through in every moment is the real reward. This is what makes your life journey truly rich and without knowing you are serving the world with your highest essence and have lived to your optimum level of being. You have now closed the gap between yourself and the divine.

Points to Remember

The reason we live a life of compromise is because we actually lack self confidence to put ourselves out there in front of the world to see what we can offer. However, this can be solved by doing the needful which will build our confidence and self esteem. Here are some steps:

Get out of Wishful Thinking	Acquire Real Skills
Gain Knowledge about Yourself	Practice Emotional Intelligence
Exercise to Build Muscle	Rely on Yourself
Eat Nutrient Dense Food	Become Efficient
Journal to Gain Mental Clarity	Learn Time Management

JOURNALING PROMPTS

How successful do you consider yourself
presently?

Do you have any unfulfilled goals?

Do you begin from a state of satisfaction or a
state of hunger, when it comes to achieving
anything in life?

The Final piece

You will be united with the one who you thought you
were separated from!
How do I know?
For I am your messenger from the heaven above.

On the uncomfortable days and the lonely nights when
you have a bed so soft but a knot so tight,
when you have amassed everything that the world says
will make you happy, peaceful and joyous,
yet in your heart you feel somethings not right.

Do not judge your life or sit in remorse,
Do not blame others or lose that last bit of hope.

There would have been no fun in this cycle of birth and
death,
had there been no stereotype to break.
Trust that you have a bigger purpose, and your place
nobody could ever take.

Now that you are here,
honour your true Guru,
the Real You.

Learn to fail and make a mistake,
learn to laugh and also allow yourself
to shed some tears.

Climb the mountains, fall in the ditch
get yourself dirty, don't fear the nasty stares.

Your five senses are your friends,
set yourself to their guidance.

In the dark of the night, when the monsters strike,
don't be afraid of that critical voice.

Slow down and clear out all the sound.
Tune in to your heart, that thumps out loud.

It says, come to me - I reside within you,
if you allow me to take the lead,
I will guide you where you were
meant to be by nature's design.

Wake up, Get up
Move Beyond Illusions

It's not just your duty
It's your Divine right!

JOURNALING PROMPT

Write a Letter To Your Greatest Fear
(recognising it will lead you towards healing)

JOURNALING PROMPT

What does healing mean for you and what does it look like?

The Benefits of using this Workbook

Having understood the basis of not being happy despite having it all, ask your self how do you intend to apply this knowledge in your life.

Do you feel that you will be able to muster up the courage to walk on your divine path. Or will you tremble? Even if you shake in the beginning and resist, it's alright because this process involves opening one's heart and pouring out all the unhelpful and unnecessary ways one has been carrying around for years. If it is too overwhelming, it's only natural. Sit with it or come back to it when you feel more comfortable and can create the space inside you to sit with these prompts.

Let's break it down and make it easier.

You do not have to chuck away your present life. The journal pages are meant for you to take this inward journey and note down everything that is important for you. Begin by taking the smallest step. Whatever feels the easiest to change, start with that.

Clarify and come back to the work book everyday.

Remove one problematic thing and add one helpful strategy. Practice the changes until you feel in control and the new habits begin to show in your behaviour, and ultimately, become your natural expression.

You may question yourself and talk yourself out of it at times. But understand this is what having lived in an illusion causes you to believe. You may also self sabotage at times.

Pause and come back.

Implement new ways of doing things in small steps.. This will give you confidence and strengthen your belief in your own decision making, slowly you will reap the benefits of joy, happiness and peace.

Each time you see yourself falling or going off track, catch yourself and lead yourself back into the lane.

Introduce more activities of your choice.

You will begin to notice that you complain less. Even when challenges arise you are able to overcome them without losing your balance.
The whole process will soon become meditative. Prosperity is now around the corner. Do not look for it or force your growth. Everything will keep falling into place day by day, month after month.

Your only role is to connect with the self every morning as you begin your day, check where any thoughts need to be addressed or corrected. Get into your inner space and operate from there. As you continue to stay connected on a consistent basis and follow your bliss instead of the dictates of the outer world, your life would have changed completely for the better when you look back. You will no longer be yearning for or expecting anything from the world outside. You will feel complete in yourself.

With regular practice, new ways of being, fresh ideas and dreams will keep erupting like the messages from Divine. These are your Blessings.

It is my hope that you find your blessings, cherish them as your precious gifts and they become the treasures that you share with the world.

9 7 9 8 8 9 4 4 6 2 0 4 2